BREAKING  FREE

FROM

ANOREXIA
&BULIMIA

Charisma
HOUSE

LINDA MINTLE, PH.D.

BREAKING FREE FROM ANOREXIA AND BULIMIA by
Linda S. Mintle, Ph.D.
Published by Charisma House
A part of Strang Communications Company
600 Rinehart Road
Lake Mary, Florida 32746
www.charismahouse.com

Unless otherwise noted, all Scripture quotations
are from the Holy Bible, New International
Version. Copyright © 1973, 1978, 1984,
International Bible Society. Used by permission.

Scripture quotations marked AMP are from the
Amplified Bible. Old Testament copyright ©
1965, 1987 by the Zondervan Corporation. The
Amplified New Testament copyright © 1954,
1958, 1987 by the Lockman Foundation. Used by
permission.

Scripture quotations marked KJV are from the
King James Version of the Bible.

Cover design by Debbie Lewis
Interior design by David Bilby

Library of Congress Catalog Card Number:
2002108796

International Standard Book Number:
0-88419-897-9

02 03 04 05 06 — 8 7 6 5 4 3 2 1
Printed in the United States of America

Quod ali cibus est aliis fuat acre venenum. (What is food to one may be fierce poison to others.)

—LUCRETIUS

CONTENTS

"I FEEL **fat**".

"When I look in the mirror, all I see is a **f a t** stomach."

"The vomiting is disgusting, but I can't stop."

"I feel so *guilty* when I eat. I need to get rid of the food."

"I WISH I COULD JUST *disappear.*"

"IT STARTED OUT AS A diet. NOW IT HAS **control** OVER ME."

"I'm so **tired** of this!"

"THIS IS **24/7**, LIKE A **nightmare** I CAN'T ESCAPE."

"I feel so ashamed."

"IF PEOPLE ONLY KNEW WHAT I DID, THEY'D *hate* ME."

"Food is controlling my life!"

INTRODUCTION

Why is it that so many of us hate our bodies? The mirror is our enemy, and we avoid it on "fat" days. We'd like better legs, fuller busts, more hair or straighter teeth. We don't feel good about ourselves because our esteem is related to body image. And when we don't feel good about ourselves, it's hard to develop meaningful relationships and move forward in life.

CAN YOU RELATE?

Mary

According to her friends, Mary had it all. Tall, thin, pretty and popular in school, no one suspected Mary was living an inner hell. Failure was something she couldn't tolerate. *If I'm not perfect, no one will like me,* she thought. Consequently, she drove herself to exhaustion. *No* was not in her vocabulary. The more she did for others, the more she neglected her own care. Her body became the object of this drive toward perfection. She had to be the thinnest. What began as a quest for perfection ended in near starvation.

Rachel

The breakup sent Rachel into a tailspin. "It's so painful to be rejected by my boyfriend. I can't believe he doesn't want to be with me anymore. Yeah, I guess I started eating to cover the pain. Now all I do is binge and throw up. I can't seem to make it stop. It's like it has taken me over. Even though I hide the vomiting, I feel so ashamed. Most of the time, I just feel numb."

Grace

"No one knows that I keep laxatives in my purse," says Grace. "At first I only took one or two every time I overate. I liked the way they cleaned out my body and took that heavy feeling away. But then I needed more because two laxatives didn't work. After awhile, I started depending on the laxatives. Whenever I overate or just ate a regular meal, I'd use them to get rid of the weight I might gain. Now I'm taking about sixty laxatives a day, and I feel so tired. My stomach hurts, and I spend my day running to the bathroom."

Rick

"It's important to have muscles and be bulked out if you are a guy," Rick tells me. "I look around the sports club, and I really have a long way to go. When I wrestled in high school, the coach told us to binge before the matches in order to make our weights. Then after the weigh-ins, we could vomit. I've started doing this binge-and-purge thing again whenever I feel I've eaten too much and haven't been able to work out. I'm getting into stacking and know it's potentially addictive. But I feel strong and in control when I'm pumping iron. My friends say I'm obsessed."

Jenna

Jenna says, "Everyone keeps telling me to just eat. I know I'm disappointing them. They have no idea how hard it is to do. My parents are tense with me, but I can't make myself eat. I look at the food and feel overwhelmed. It's scary, so I just push the food around on my plate. They tell me I look too thin, but I don't see it. I feel fat. I'm not in any danger. I can control this. I'll start eating more soon. Please don't be upset with me."

Jenna was a sweet girl, known for doing the right thing. How was it, then, that this highly responsible teen became so angry when you mentioned her eating problem? Any talk of her dangerously low weight or food restriction was met with vehement denial. It didn't seem to matter what people said. Jenna refused to eat more than a couple of bites of salad and rice. Jenna would not admit to having an eating disorder, even though she exhibited all the classic signs.

We've been deceived into thinking the body is the key to happiness and fulfillment.

THIN IS IN

Magazines keep us knowledgeable about the latest dieting fads, and then they tempt us with exotic cuisine that even the strongest can't resist. Plastic surgeons suggest we take action against those specific body parts we don't like. Models keep getting thinner despite our ever-growing concern about eating disorders. Women still go on dates and salivate over the steak he's eating while trying to enjoy the light salad she ordered. You know it's true—men find women who eat small meals on dates more attractive and more feminine. It's crazy!

When I talk to men and women, more than half of both genders would choose a different body. And they don't want to wait until they get to heaven to have it! People are willing to try anything—medications, hypnosis, fad diets, liquid diets, surgery—whatever it takes to approximate that fashion model look.

We've been deceived into thinking the body is the key to happiness and fulfillment. "The perfect body will bring us everything we need." What a lie, but we swallow it. And when life feels out of control, controlling your body brings a false sense of control.

It's time to break free from the bondage

of anorexia and bulimia. In this book, you will:

- Learn how to recognize anorexia and bulimia

- Understand the physical, emotional, relational and spiritual impact of eating disorders

- Learn how eating disorders develop

- Uncover deception and learn biblical truth

- Be given break-free strategies

- Move into freedom

BREAKING FREE
PRAYER FOR YOU

Food has become an obsession with me. All I think about is eating and not eating. I weigh myself all the time. My mood depends on what I weigh. I know this isn't right. Lord, help me break free.

CHAPTER 1

WHAT ARE EATING DISORDERS?

A "snapshot" feature in USA Today *listed the five greatest concerns parents and teachers had about children in the fifties: talking out of turn, chewing gum in class, doing homework, stepping out of line, cleaning their rooms. Then it listed the five top concerns of parents today: drug addiction, teenage pregnancy, suicide and homicide, gang violence, anorexia and bulimia. We can also add AIDS, poverty, and homelessness... Between my own childhood and the advent of my motherhood—one short*

generation—the culture had
gone completely mad.[1]
—MARY KAY BLAKELY
AUTHOR AND MOTHER

We all diet now and then. But dieting can become a way of life or, worse yet, an obsession that prevents you from enjoying life. In fact, you may find yourself wondering if you have a problem when it comes to food, weight and body issues. Do you constantly think about your weight and what goes in your mouth? Does the number on the scale determine your happiness?

BREAKING FREE
MENTAL HEALTH FACT

Food and Me

If you think you may have a problem when it comes to eating, ask yourself these fifteen questions:

1. Do I constantly think about food, my body or my weight?

2. Does the thought of eating make me feel anxious?

3. Am I afraid I'll get fat?

4. Do I keep eating when I'm not physically hungry?

5. Am I having trouble eating and don't know what physical hunger is?

6. Do I eat until I feel sick?

7. Do I weigh myself several times a day or week?

8. Am I upset if I miss exercising?

9. Do I think that controlling the food portions I eat makes me a better person?

10. Do I make myself throw up after I've eaten?

11. Have I taken laxatives to lose weight?

12. Do I use weight loss products?

13. Do I feel like food has taken control of me?

14. Do I eat when I feel unpleasant emotions?

15. Do I hate my body?

If you answered *yes* to a number of these questions, you may have an eating disorder or show early signs of developing one. The sooner you do something about your attitudes and feelings toward food, the more you can avoid falling prey to unhealthy patterns.

AN OBSESSED CULTURE

The emphasis on beauty and weight in our culture is out of balance. It seems that everywhere we turn we are bombarded by media images of the perfect-looking man or woman. The onslaught of *thin is in* has contributed to the growing number of girls and guys obsessed with attaining the perfect body.

Perhaps you have seen pictures of emaciated women who think they are fat or watched news magazine shows that report stories about girls who slowly starve themselves to near death. Models, actresses and ballet dancers are well known for having high numbers of anorexic people in their professions—professions in which body shape and appearance are of great importance.

You probably know someone who has or had an eating disorder. If you live in a college dorm, you don't have to look far because it is rampant on our campuses.

Eating disorders are serious and usually require treatment by a mental health multidisciplinary team. Even though they are primarily of psychological origin, they involve medical and physical complications. Early intervention is best because of the potential for serious medical problems, the extreme being death. These disorders affect men and women of all ages, but are especially present in young women. Adolescents are most at risk, but all ages can be affected.

ABNORMAL EATING

Abnormal eating patterns may include self-starvation, compulsive eating and self-induced purging. Simple starvation leads to anorexia nervosa; binge eating and purging to bulimia nervosa. In some cases, people have a combination of anorexic and bulimic symptoms.

Both disorders share in common certain symptoms: intense fear of gaining weight, excessive preoccupation with food and eating, chronic dieting, poor body image, depression and the need for approval by others.

ANOREXIA

Anorexia involves severe weight loss, excessive exercise, body image disturbance, fear of getting fat and food avoidance. Just under 1 percent of adolescent girls develop this disorder. Since about 90 percent of anorexics are girls, it is primarily a female problem.[2]

Someone with anorexia will begin to make rigid rules about eating and food. For example, she will label some foods "bad" and avoid them. Or she may claim to be vegetarian without any real knowledge of a vegetarian diet. A number of the girls I've treated use "vegetarian diet" as a code word for only eating salads and avoiding meat. Others become vegetarians before they begin losing significant weight.

In addition to selecting only certain foods

deemed "good," anorexics will chew food slowly numerous times. Food is cut up into small bites and moved around the plate to give the appearance of eating. A fear of food accompanies a fear of weight gain. Thus, there is usually

Secrecy and denial are common with both anorexia and bulimia.

a tendency to exercise excessively or to take laxatives, water pills, diet pills or to vomit as a way to keep from gaining weight. However, not all anorexics purge in these ways. Those who do purge are at even greater risk given their already emaciated physical state. A purging episode can be fatal and increase the risk of cardiac arrest.

Secrecy and denial are common with both anorexia and bulimia. As a girl loses weight, she may wear baggy clothes in order to hide her thin state. Typically, she feels that others are judging her by what she eats, so she avoids eating in front of people. Thoughts of food, weight and body image are intrusive. The more she can control her food intake, the better she feels. Weighing food and counting calories are common. A small or regular-size meal looks overwhelming. Eating it would lead to feeling uncomfortable and guilty. After a meal of any size, there is usually a wish to weigh on the scale. Actually jumping on the scale may occur multiple times a day.

BREAKING  F R E E

MENTAL HEALTH FACT

Signs of Anorexia

- Weight loss and refusal to gain to normal weight (a weight loss of 15 percent below an acceptable weight)

- Intense fear of becoming fat or gaining weight

- Body image disturbance

- Loss of menses in females—three consecutive cycles[3]

Other signs to look for are feelings of worthlessness and hopelessness, fatigue and signs of depression, which include loss of interest in things, poor concentration, irritability, agitation, restlessness, with-drawal, a down mood, sleep problems and suicidal thoughts.

PHYSICAL AND MEDICAL COMPLICATIONS OF ANOREXIA

Since anorexia involves self-starvation, it can cause a number of physical and medical problems.

BREAKING FREE

MENTAL HEALTH FACT

Physical and Medical Complications of Anorexia

- Loss of menses (amenorrhea)
- Dry skin and hair
- Cold hands and feet
- Weakness
- Constipation
- Digestive problems
- An increase in infections
- Ketosis
- Osteoporosis
- Irregular heartbeat and heart failure
- Mild anemia
- Swollen joints

- Low blood pressure
- Muscle wasting
- Lanugo (growth of fine hair on the body)
- Headaches
- Concentration problems
- Fainting[4]

BULIMIA

In recent years people have talked openly about bulimia. You may have heard Tracey Gold (*Growing Pains*), gymnast Cathy Rigby, pop star Ginger Spice, actress Jane Fonda or the most famous bulimic, Princess Diana, speak out about their secret obsession. Why don't more women and men speak up? It's embarrassing to tell people you eat in an out-of-control way and then throw up. Shame is a big silencer.

Bulimia is an eating disorder characterized by binge-purge cycles. During a binge, large amounts of food are consumed while feeling out of control. Typically, foods high in sugars or carbohydrates are chosen. Because of the high number of calories consumed, the stomach hurts. Purging usually follows. Many methods of purging (getting rid of the food) are used. These methods include vomiting, taking laxatives, diuretics (water pills), diet pills, exercising excessively, using enemas, fasting or drinking Ipecac syrup to induce vomiting.

BREAKING FREE

MENTAL HEALTH FACT

Signs of Bulimia

- Bingeing and purging occur at least twice a week for a three-month period

- Obsession with body weight and shape

- Feeling out of control and fear of gaining weight

- Purging (see above) to compensate for binges[5]

~~~~~~~~~~

Unlike anorexics, you can't easily spot a bulimic because she is usually at normal weight. But weight loss and gain can fluctuate. And because there is so much secrecy associated with bingeing and purging, families and friends can be fooled into thinking eating is normal. For example, a teen may eat her meal and then excuse herself to the bathroom. In the bathroom, she'll run the fan, vomit, clean it up and spray air freshener. Behind the cover-up, however, are feelings of shame and guilt.

B R E A K I N G F R E E

M E N T A L   H E A L T H F A C T

Physical and Medical Complications of Bulimia

Bulimia can bring on medical problems such as:

- Stomach or esophagi rupture (rare, but it happens)

- Heart irregularities due to loss of vital minerals such as potassium

- Wearing away of the enamel on teeth from acid when vomiting

- Scarring on the backs of hands from using fingers to induce vomiting

- Inflamed esophagus
- Swollen glands and puffy cheeks
- Irregular menstrual periods
- Diminished interest in sex
- Intestinal problems due to constant irritation of the colon from laxative abuse
- Kidney problems from abuse of diuretics
- Dehydration and electrolyte imbalance
- "Insulin dumping" in which high amounts of sugary foods are eaten and the pancreas releases large amounts of insulin[6]

~~~~~~~~

This disorder usually begins in adolescence and is related to intense feelings of being out of control. While food is the substance used to numb emotional pain and difficulty, underlying issues must be faced. Food is often used as a coping mechanism for anger, anxiety, depression and stress related to many areas of young women's lives. The longer you wait to get help, the more ingrained the habit becomes.

MALES WITH EATING DISORDERS

Not much media attention is given to men and eating disorders. One reason may be that these disorders are disproportionately female. Out of the approximately 8 million who suffer eating disorders, about 10 percent are men.[7] In recent years, however, the number of males afflicted has risen.

Men, like women, are affected by cultural media stereotypes that promote a fit and buffed body as a sign of attractiveness and success. But men are more concerned about their shape than weight. Men are also affected by other sociocultural factors such as the pressure of a demanding job market and the changing view of masculinity and gender roles.

The longer you wait to get help, the more ingrained the habit becomes.

Exercise appears to be a common entrée into symptom development. Dieting plays a role related to playing sports, past obe-

14

sity, gender identity conflicts and avoidance of feared medical illness. Boys may begin to diet to lose a few pounds, exercise to lose more weight and then refuse to eat normally. Exercise is usually the chosen route for weight loss.

Like women, certain subgroups of men are more at risk. Male wrestlers have a high proportion of eating disorders. Approximately one-fourth of all male cases of eating disorders is found among men with homosexual orientation. In addition, men who develop eating disorders are more likely than women to have been obese.[8]

Clinical symptoms in males are similar, with the obvious exception of amenorrhea. Onset of a male eating disorder can begin at preadolescence, adolescence, young adulthood or adulthood. Men benefit greatly from treatment and are often happy to find someone who appreciates their concerns.

Why are these disorders more typically female? One thought is that males don't diet as often to control weight. In addition, males increase muscle during puberty and are less concerned about fat than girls. Males want to be bigger and taller. It also may be that eating disorders in males are underdiagnosed and underreported since they are known as female disorders.

Whatever the reasons, it is important to know that some males use food to cope with emotional difficulties and are at risk.

What Causes Eating Disorders?

So what causes eating disorders? This easy question has a complex answer. Families are mystified as to what makes a sixteen-year-old girl jeopardize her health. Friends are disgusted by the vomiting sounds heard in college dorm bathrooms. Husbands are baffled by the seeming inability of their wives to love themselves. Why do women and men abuse their bodies with food? Researchers search for answers.

There is no one thing that predicts whether someone will submit to the bondage of these disorders. What we do know is that the causes are multiple, inter-active and complex. No one factor stands alone. Keeping that in mind, and knowing that we don't have definitive answers, here are some of the risk factors thought to lead to the predisposition and development of an eating disorder.

BREAKING 🦅 F R E E

MENTAL HEALTH FACT

Risk Factors

- History of a mood disorder (increased risk for bulimia) or family history of mood disorder

- Traumatic life events

- Difficulty coping with stress

- Dysfunctional family or other relationships

- Low self-esteem

- Dissatisfaction with looks

- Genetics: Eating disorders do tend to run in families. Usually females are most affected. This may suggest that some people are predisposed to these disorders, but it certainly doesn't eliminate the role other factors play. Research is currently being conducted to look carefully at the role of genetics.

- Family history of substance abuse may increase the risk for bulimia.

- Odd family eating habits and strong concern about appearance and weight may translate to family members.

- Dissatisfaction with body and desire to be thin

- Dieting appears to be an entrée to an eating disorder.

- Normal development events such as the onset of puberty, leaving home or the beginning of a new relationship, particularly with the opposite sex

- Repeated negative comments on appearance

- Emphasis on thinness among upper- and middle-class women and female adolescents

- Positive family history of eating disorders coupled with dieting

- Personality traits: In girls who

develop anorexia, there is a tendency to overly control emotions and be emotionally intolerant. In addition, there is often a lack of self-direction and difficulty adapting to developmental tasks. In the development of bulimia, girls tend to have unstable emotions and poor impulse control.

- Being in a sport or athletic program that emphasized a certain body type or image (ballet, gymnastics, swimming, wrestling, etc.)

- Difficulty dealing with negative emotions and regulating them[9]

As you can see, many things can influence the development of eating disorders—the tremendous cultural pressure to be thin and beautiful, gender role expectations and changes, family patterns, personality factors, physiological predispositions and experience around loss, abuse and other trauma. There are no simple answers.

It's Not Just About Food

I know they are called *eating disorders*, but it should be obvious by now that they are not just about food. Dieting and weight focus may be an obvious beginning to an eating disorder, but there is much more involved. Otherwise, we'd all have eating disorders!

Most eating disorders emerge around the time of puberty and when a young adult prepares to leave home. These are developmental times of stress. As a child's body changes and she is faced with emerging sexuality and pressure to develop her own identity, she may find herself obsessing on food as a way to control feelings that seem out of control.

Another time of intense stress is during the time of developmental launching, which usually begins in high school and continues as teens move out to attend college or enter the job market. This developmental transition requires independence and firming up of identity. When a teen feels highly dependent on others to take care of her or unsure of her personal identity, she is at risk for an eating disorder to develop.

Family members are often frightened by the eating behavior because of the seriousness of related medical problems and because the person is misusing food. People with eating disorders often try to take care of family members or other people in their lives while denying their own needs and care. It is easier to focus on making other people happy than to do the hard work of self-examination.

Although each case is different, there are common family patterns seen in treatment. Typically, but not in all cases, fathers are emotionally uninvolved and disconnected to their daughters; mothers are overinvolved or underinvolved; and siblings are not connected as a group. The overinvolvement of mothers gets a bad rap. Mothers are the ones who usually notice the problem and stay on top of getting help. In many families, moms are more emotionally connected to their daughters than their husbands. Because the fathers tend to pull back from emotional connection as the daughter matures, mothers become more involved. Siblings often feel left out as all the attention goes to the child with the eating problem. So you can see, working on *all* family relationships is important.

Common areas of family problems are difficulty communicating or directly managing conflict and handling negative emotions. In many cases, there is marital conflict, and the child with the eating disorder becomes the peacemaker or deflector of that tension.

Working on all family relationships is important.

In families with an anorexic, little emotion is directly expressed. Family conflict is denied, and the child tries to be perfect. In bulimic families, problems aren't denied; they just aren't resolved. Eating symptoms are unsuccessful attempts to control and resolve problems.

Parenting is often done in extreme fashion—overprotective or chaotic. This results in the child feeling guilty, overwhelmed and lonely, and avoiding her need to separate developmentally and face the challenges of growing up. Eating disorders are a desperate attempt to push away from the family system. The young woman wants to grow up, but at the same time she is frightened and feels unprepared to do so. Eating problems keep her family involved in caretaking her.

Life for someone with an eating disorder is often lived in the extremes—it's all or nothing. There are no in-betweens or moderation when it comes to dealing with people, food, emotions or even God for that matter.

TAGALONGS

In so many cases, eating disorders coexist with other emotional problems. We call these "tagalong" conditions. They are depression, anxiety, obsessive-compulsive behavior, posttraumatic stress and other personality disorders. In addition to these conditions, sexual abuse and substance abuse are commonly found with bulimia.[10]

Because mood, thinking and behavior are all affected by starvation, one has to determine whether these conditions resulted from the eating disorder or whether they were present before the eating problems began. Either way, they must be addressed. For example, if you experienced date rape and developed bulimia six months later, it would be important to treat the trauma related to the rape in addition to treating the eating problems. Most likely the trauma is where problems began.

SPIRITUAL DECEPTION

Spiritual deception is always present. It has to be in order for someone to look in a mirror and not see the wasting away of the body or to believe there is no danger when all signs point to a serious problem. If the enemy can get you to believe you are only as good as others say, or that your performance and accomplishments determine who you are, he can deceive you into thinking you control your own life and destiny.

Your identity is not found in what you do or how you look.

The truth is that you have no real control, and nothing you do changes this fact. God is in control of all things. You don't impress God with your performance. Nothing you do earns His free gift of salvation and His Spirit living inside of you. Your identity is not found in what you do or how you look.

This is actually great news because it relieves you of tremendous pressure. God wants you to surrender to His love and to know Him intimately. Surrender is the key. Then He can heal you and more clearly direct your path. But you have to let Him.

BREAKING FREE

PRAYER FOR YOU

Lord, I know I've been thinking more about food than about You. Food seems to preoccupy most of my thoughts, and I want to be free of this. I feel so unsure of myself except when I control my food intake—I'm good at that! The rest of my life feels out of control and frightening. Help me to surrender to You. I now realize that whatever control I thought I had is false.

CHAPTER 2

HOUSTON, WE HAVE A PROBLEM!

*No one can make you inferior
without your consent.*
— ELEANOR ROOSEVELT

One of the biggest obstacles to healing is breaking through the denial of the eating problem. Many of you don't believe you are harming yourselves. Nothing anyone can say will convince you otherwise.

The power of denial is so strong you will risk your life to stay in control of food. This over control eventually results in being out of control. You can no longer eat normally. But even then, the problem is denied. "Oh, I can start eating right when I want to." Or, "I promise. I'll gain weight tomorrow." The threat of danger is not motivating. You falsely believe in your own ability to find a solution. So far you haven't, but you are not giving up. You have to take control of your life. Right now, that is through food and eating.

This powerful denial is rooted, I believe, in spiritual deception. Since the enemy's purpose is to steal, kill and then destroy, we know he'd like nothing better than to deceive you into thinking everything is OK when it's not. He whispers, "Take control. You decide what to eat and when. If you want it, indulge. You can always get rid of it. You won't get hurt by this."

Remember Eve's mistake. She was deceived by the serpent. She listened to him lie about eating. He hates you as much as he did Eve. You, the image of God, must be destroyed. So he plays the same game. Eat the fruit, and the pizza, the chips, the doughnuts, the cake, the ice cream…then throw it up. No harm will come to you.

Then he plays on your emotions and wants you to think like this, *I don't want to feel pain. I can control what I eat even though I can't control other things in my life. If I'm perfect with food, I'll feel better about myself. I can learn to ignore hunger.*

This makes me feel superior and in control. I must be thinner than everyone else. Thin is happy. Self-denial is good. I can be perfect if I try hard enough. When I think about food, I don't have to think about painful and difficult things—my family relationships, men, growing up, being independent.

As you begin to lose weight, you are complimented. After significant weight loss, worry replaces compliments. But you don't see the problem. You are convinced that self-control is necessary. Self-denial becomes an idol. You feel self-righteous through restricting food.

Denial continues to push away painful feelings. It is a defensive process that allows you to keep pretending nothing is

Denial redirects underlying emotional, psychological and spiritual problems to the body.

wrong. Denial helps avoid negative emotions and experiences. If you admit to negative feelings, you are weak. By now, you can't even get in touch with the pain. It won't surface. It's buried somewhere down deep. Food control covers it up.

Denial redirects underlying emotional, psychological and spiritual problems to the body. An illusion of power is created—the more self-denial, the more special you become. Your "specialness" results in people needing to take care of you. But you want to take care of yourself. Admitting you need help means giving control to someone else. Giving control to others is frightening. In the past, it meant loneliness or pain. Can't go there or do that!

CONFRONT DENIAL

Breaking through denial is often a slow process, one that develops through trust and relationships with people who care.

Admitting to anorexia or bulimia often requires a step of faith. You don't see the problem, but you must believe what others say is true. Believing something you can't see is faith. It sounds like an easy step, but it isn't. Most people with an eating disorder adamantly deny it. Confronting denial is the first step in healing.

You have allowed yourself to be

deceived into thinking you are OK. As long as you hold on to this thought, you won't feel sick. You may even have physical symptoms and still tell yourself that you are OK. Feelings are unpredictable. That's why we don't rely on feelings.

If someone is telling you that you have a problem, let go of your pride and believe him or her. It doesn't matter what you feel; embrace truth. Make a mental decision to admit to the problem. Then, by faith, accept the need for help. Every time your head tells you that you are not struggling, say, "That's a lie. I have a problem. Here is the evidence. (List off the symptoms others see.) Until I admit it, I won't get better." Say this every day if you have to. Say it at every meal. Stay in the reality of the situation. Your mind will try to trick you into thinking you are OK when you are not. Ask God to speak His truth to you. It's the voice of the enemy who lies.

Your tendency will be to not trust others. Other people have been a source of pain and hurt. You have learned to push negative feelings deep down inside. You are too frightened to trust. Trusting someone who wants to help you is essential. Accept help no matter how scary it feels. You must be willing to give up total control.

Spiritually, you must repent. You have depended on yourself to a fault. You have not allowed God to help you because you feel you failed Him. This is another lie. We've all failed God a thousand times. But His mercy is so great. You can't be perfect for Him. Even if you could,

> *Letting go is an act of faith. It's the only way to begin the process of healing.*

that's not what His love is all about. He wants you just as you are—weak, failed and in need. Then He can be strong. Let Him make you whole and functioning to full capacity. He promised you a sound mind. Your body is not a temple to be worshiped; it's the place where His Spirit lives. He wants to live in a well place.

Letting go is an act of faith. It's the only way to begin the process of healing. Will you admit to the problem? Will you take a step of faith? Will you acknowledge your need for Jesus to be Lord of all? Will you give up control and be dependent on Him?

"I Can Will Myself Better"

Another block to healing is the belief that you can somehow will yourself better. If you just try harder... This is the mantra of our modern-day psychology. It's all about us and what we can do to make ourselves happy and well. How misguided this is! And yet, it is purported in books, on television shows and in the media. The power of you. It's inside you. You have what it takes to heal yourself.

When you are in bondage to anything, you need the healing power of Jesus. He alone is able to set you free. You can work yourself to your emaciated bone and still not experience freedom. Why? Because you can't do it in your own power. Turn to Him. He won't disappoint.

Stop Minimizing

You can't get well if you believe that what you are doing is not a big deal. Your behavior is dangerous. It can cause physical sickness, relationship problems, internal agony and spiritual numbness; it can even lead to your death. No other psychiatric disorder has a higher morbidity or mortality rate.[1] That's a chilling fact.

It's time to trust those around you who say you have a problem. I know it's scary, because giving up this eating disorder identity means finding another. But that's just the point. You already have an identity that's healthy. You just have to learn about it and embrace it. And it has nothing to do with anything you do or how you look!

BREAKING FREE

PRAYER FOR YOU

Lord, I admit I have a problem. All I can think about is food and my body. I'm afraid of gaining weight, and yet I know fear is not from you. I want to break the strongholds that keep me bound and be free. I'm tired of feeling this way. I'm tired of trying to do things on my own. I need Your help. Forgive my pride. I invite You into the process.

CHAPTER 3

BIBLICAL GUIDANCE

A life lived listening to the decisive call of God is a life lived before one audience that trumps all others—the Audience of One.

—OS GUINNESS FROM
THE CALL (1998)

*T*he Bible talks about eating. It is a natural part of our everyday life. Food is enjoyable and necessary to good health. It is not a sin to enjoy a good meal. So to deny yourself that pleasure (unless you are fasting for spiritual reasons) is senseless.

The problem comes when food takes on meaning other than that intended by God. Food should not become an idol or a source of worry. Matthew 6:25 specifically tells us not to worry about what we eat or drink or worry about our bodies. Why?

Because eating is a need that God will supply. He made provision in the Garden of Eden, gave instructions for the food supply in Noah's ark, rained down food from heaven in the wilderness and fed the very hungry five thousand with loaves and fishes. Throughout the Bible, God supplies food to sustain and nourish His own. And His promises are the same yesterday, today and forever.

In addition to meeting our physical needs, God wants to satisfy our spiritual appetite as well. In John 6:35 He calls Himself the *Bread of Life*. He says that whoever comes to Him will never be thirsty or hungry again. What a promise! He will fulfill *all* our longings and hunger.

You are probably saying, "Great, but how does this relate to an eating disorder?" God created us to hunger in the natural and spiritual. An eating disorder is a false attempt to satisfy both hungers. Eating and its enjoyment are denied by the

Emotional hunger is tied to a need for affirmation and identity.

anorexic. The bulimic overindulges and then wreaks havoc on the body trying to eliminate the food. Food is neither enjoyed nor used properly to nourish the body.

Emotional hunger is tied to a need for affirmation and identity. This need is God given, but the fulfillment comes from Him. An eating disorder is a failed attempt to be affirmed (through thinness) by others and to find an identity separate from Christ. Someone with an eating disorder buys the culture's prescription for identity—beauty, thinness, fame, success, achievement, perfection and so on. However, none of these things ultimately satisfy. Only God can fill that empty place by awakening your true identity and affirming you in Him.

So the first biblical prescription is to know who you are in Christ. He chose you, not based on anything you did to deserve it, but based on his unmerited favor. He highly esteems you because you are created in His image. He desires you.

For most of you reading this, this sounds too easy. *I don't have to do anything to be loved by God? I don't have to look a certain way? I can make mistakes, and He forgives me? I don't have to be perfect? He wants to bless me and give me good things? He chose me because He loves me? I don't have any relationships like this.* Well, guess what? You do. You just didn't know it. God's been waiting for you to come around and get to know Him—intimately. He wants you. You won't find anyone or anything like His love. Stop resisting. Give in to His call.

In addition, you have to stop disbelieving what He says about you. Maybe you don't *feel* what He says is true. OK, but don't go by feelings. Go by what you know to be true (the Word of God). By faith believe it. If the problem is that the enemy has implanted lies about who you are, ask God to reveal His truth to you. He will.

B R E A K I N G F R E E

M E N T A L H E A L T H F A C T

Who You Are in Christ

In order to know who you are in Christ, read the Bible and pull out all the scriptures that talk about your identity and your acceptance. There are so many. Here are just a few:

Psalm 139:14	You are wonderful. You are fearfully and wonderfully made.
John 1:12	You are God's child.
John 3:16	God loves you just the way you are.
John 15:15	As a disciple, you are a friend of Jesus Christ.
1 Corinthians 6:19–20	You have been bought with a price and belong to God.
1 Corinthians 12:27	You are a member of Christ's body.
Ephesians 1:3–8	You have been chosen by God and adopted as His child.
Philippians 4:19	God will supply all your needs.
Colossians 1:13–14	You have been redeemed and for-

	given of all your sins.
Colossians 2:9–10	You are complete in Christ.

~~~~~~~~~~

If you need more help to develop a healthy God image and better understand your true identity, I recommend you read *Breaking Free From a Negative Self-Image.*[1] In that book, I go into much more detail on developing God esteem and finding your identity in Christ.

DEPEND ON GOD

You are probably reluctant to depend on God. Because people let you down, you are convinced God will do the same. Therefore, you think you must be self-sufficient. Anorexia and bulimia are misguided attempts to be self-sufficient. And self-sufficiency doesn't please God. Basically, the self-sufficient person says, "I don't need Jesus and what He did for me. The cross was great, but it wasn't enough to help me. Thanks, but no thanks." Think about it.

Let go of the old self or false self and gain new life through Christ. He has great plans for you if you allow Him to be Lord of all. But you must desire Him to take His place. It isn't enough to have good intentions about God. You must want to be healed and depend on God to do a complete work in you. He's totally able to heal you, but He wants your cooperation. Surrender to His love. You won't be disappointed.

THE STRUGGLE TO BE FREE

The struggle involved in breaking free from an eating disorder is found in Romans 7:15–20. It describes the cry of so many women's hearts.

Look carefully at this passage. If possible, read it from the Amplified Bible. Paul says we have the intention of doing right (sound familiar?) but no power to carry it out. Our flesh fails us. No list of food rules, eating regulations, diets, restrictions or other thing is going to make you healthy. You can't overcome this in your

> *Surrender to His love. You won't be disappointed.*

own power. Apart from Christ working in you, you are powerless to conquer this thing.

Repent from trying to act in your own strength. Your efforts will continue to fail. Ask Him to give you the power to overcome. Begin to praise Him for who He is and what He has done for you. The victory is won. God doesn't lose. He can set you free.

Every day, praise and worship Him, read His Word, renew your mind with the promises of God, have faith, put on your royal garments—you are royalty, a joint heir with Christ. Take your rightful position as His daughter. And loose those chains of bondage. It's not through your own efforts and sets of rules, but through the Holy Spirit in you, empowering you to be who God intended you to be.

LIVE TO PLEASE GOD, NOT OTHERS

When you have an eating disorder, you spend so much time and energy trying to please everyone. It's a never-ending battle that leaves you exhausted. It's time to stop this misguided effort. You only have to please God. Read 1 Thessalonians 4. The entire chapter is a powerful description of what pleases God. There is no other audience to please. Only the "Audience of One," as Os Guinness so eloquently reminds us. Read this. Meditate on it and let it sink into your spirit.

BREAKING F R E E

MENTAL HEALTH FACT

Bible Truths to Help

Here are bits of biblical truth that will help you:

- If we are controlled by our sinful nature, we can't please God (Rom. 8:8).

- God is the only one you must please. If your aim is to please men, Scripture says that you aren't a servant of Christ (Gal. 1:10).

- Grow in the knowledge of God: "And we pray this in order that you may live a life worthy of the Lord and may please him in every way: bearing fruit in every good work, growing in the knowledge of God" (Col. 1:10).

- His Spirit lives in you. "For God was pleased to have all his fullness dwell in him" (Col. 1:19).

- God sees your heart. "On the contrary, we speak as men approved by God to be entrusted with the gospel. We are not trying to please men but God, who tests our hearts" (1 Thess. 2:4).

- Faith is needed. "And without faith it is impossible to please God, because anyone who comes to him must believe that he exists and that he rewards those who earnestly seek him" (Heb. 11:6).

~~~~~~~~~~

PRESENT YOUR BODY TO CHRIST

It is the enemy's plan to have you sin against your body. If you confess Christ as your Savior, your body is the dwelling place of the Holy Spirit (1 Cor. 3:16).

Satan hates that and wants your body destroyed. It's the closest thing he can do to defile you because he can no longer inhabit you. So he torments you with thoughts like, *You are unclean. Look what you do to your body. You may be forgiven, but you are disgusting.*

When an eating disorder is active, you do secretive things with your body—vomit, take laxatives, binge and so on. These secrets are a playground in which Satan can work. He loves the darkness and floods you with shame. If he can get you to feel you are unclean, he has a foothold.

The way out of this trap is to bring all things to the Light—the light of Christ. Your body is for the Lord. Refuse to be brought under the power of anything—shame, food or ungodly thoughts (1 Cor. 6:12). Renounce the hidden things of shame (2 Cor. 4:2). Repent from comparing yourself and measuring yourself against others (2 Cor. 10:12). Present your body as a living sacrifice, holy and acceptable to God (Rom. 12:1).

APPLY THE WORD

Women I've treated tell me the same thing over and over: "I know scriptures should change my thinking, but they don't." Or, "I cry as a response to an awesome promise of God, but it doesn't seem to change me in the long run. Why is this?"

It's one thing to *know* a truth in your head or even *feel* a truth in your emotions, but it's another to let that truth sink into your mind and renew it. We must invite God's Word to have complete authority over our emotions. Otherwise, we respond like the wind, feeling this and that, but never allowing God to do the deep work involved in complete surrender.

Ask God to let His Word penetrate deep within you. He will give you revelation if you meditate on it and use it as food for your soul. Allow God to transform every part of you, not just your problems. Give your entire life, all your thoughts and emotions to Him. When He has complete authority over you because you invite Him to do so, your life will be changed.

P R A Y E R   F O R   Y O U

Forgive me, Lord, for trying to act in my own power. It doesn't work. I need You. I can't break free without Your help. Now I will depend on You. I will read Your Word to learn my true identity and be affirmed by You. I want to be a God pleaser, not a man pleaser. I present my body as a living sacrifice to You. I will stop defiling it and give You free reign to shine the light of Your truth in all parts of me. Let nothing hidden stay hidden. It's only when I bring all things into the light that I will be healed.

CHAPTER 4

WORKING WITH A TEAM

Habit is habit and not to be flung out of the window by any man, but coaxed downstairs a step at a time.

—MARK TWAIN

God is our healer. He can do miraculous things. I have no doubt that He can touch you and make you whole because of who He is. It has been my experience that healing, for many with these disorders, comes progressively. I believe this is because God wants all the parts involved in creating these disorders to be healed.

Because these disorders affect the physical, emotional, cognitive and spiritual dimensions of a person, you may need the help of other people in order to break free. There are several key players who may be involved. Let's talk about them and why they are important to your health.

Most of us are hesitant to seek help even when we think we may need it. However, a therapist or a counselor can be instrumental in breaking free. Choosing a therapist is difficult to do. It's not like getting a new car or shopping for handbags. You want someone who is caring, empathetic, who listens to you and understands you. Above that, you want someone who is competent, knows the field of eating disorders, has experience, lives the Christian faith and understands that our weapons of warfare are mighty in God. Does this sound like a tall order? It is, but God has equipped others to help you.

So who are the players that may be involved in helping you?

A psychiatrist is a medical doctor who can prescribe medications as a part of treatment if needed. Most nonmedical therapists work with a physician, should the need for evaluation and prescription arise. Medication is not a given in treating these disorders. Many people are treated without medication.

Qualified therapists can be found through asking family doctors, mental health clinics, college counselors, women's resource centers, school nurses, employee assistance programs, church staffs, ministers and other professionals who treat or cross paths with eating disorder patients. Ask around. Ask people who have had a good experience with a particular counselor for a referral.

Also check national resources for referrals in your local area. Don't be afraid to ask for a Christian therapist. Many hospitals, insurance companies and referral sources keep provider information about therapists who are listed as "Christian."

BREAKING FREE
MENTAL HEALTH FACT

Choosing a Therapist

When choosing a therapist, I recommend you ask these ten questions:

1. Does the therapist have training and experience with this specialty population?

2. Does the therapist have access to other multidisciplinary team members like physicians, dietitians or exercise physiologists?

3. Will the therapist work in concert with other members of the multidisciplinary team so that all your needs are addressed?

4. Will your weight and physical health be checked on a regular basis?

5. What are the therapist's plans for care, including number of sessions, treatment approach, involvement of the family and level of care?

6. Does the therapist integrate Christianity into the treatment? If so, how?

7. Is the therapist knowledgeable about current eating disorders, treatments and research?

8. Has the therapist been successful in guiding others to overcome eating disorders?

9. How does the therapist view the role of medications?

10. Does the therapist believe recovery is possible, but that freedom can be achieved through the power of Jesus Christ?

~~~~~~~~

It is best to get help quickly. Treatment can save your life! The longer you stay in your abnormal eating habits, the more ingrained they become. The first step back to health is to have a complete physical exam by a physician who understands the medical issues involved with eating disorders. He or she will need to rule out any possible physical causes for the disorder and check your current medical condition.

Most people can be treated in an outpatient setting, but sometimes hospitalization is necessary. Hospitalization is usually considered when weight loss is severe, when there are serious metabolic disturbances, when there is a risk of suicide due to clinical depression, when outpatient has failed, when bingeing and

You need a comprehensive plan that will help you break free from the disorder.

purging is severe or with someone experiencing psychosis.

Because eating disorders involve complex emotional, psychological and spiritual issues, you need a comprehensive plan that will help you break free from the disorder. Usually a team of professionals is assembled to treat you. Remember, the goal is *freedom*, not recovery. Here is a brief description of the role various professionals can play.

A medical doctor (M.D.)

Because of the serious medical and physical conditions associated with eating problems, you need a physician who will monitor your physical state. For a child or young teen, a pediatrician is a good choice. For older women and men, find an internist or family practice doctor. He or she will monitor blood work, your weight and examine you regularly. As noted above, a complete physical is recommended.

A registered dietitian (R.D.)

This person will work with you on food choices, calorie intake and eating habits. I know so many of you could write books on calories and eating. But it's one thing to be knowledgeable about food and another to apply that knowledge to your own life. A registered dietitian may ask you to keep a food journal for a few weeks so the two of you can look at your food choices. You may need to add variety to your meal plan, eat at more regular times, eat less or make other changes. Accountability with a registered dietitian is helpful even when you think you know all about food choices.

In addition, the dietitian and physician can work together to establish a healthy weight for you. Left to your own ideas, your weight goal is often too low or unreasonable. The dietitian will supervise your food intake and bring accountability to your choices and habits. She will help establish good eating habits, correct faulty information about food and help you gain or lose the appropriate amount of weight safely and sensibly. The emphasis is on teaching you to use food as nutrition, not as a coping mechanism. If you are underweight, it is also her job to encourage you to reach your target weight.

An exercise physiologist

If you need help with safe and appropriate exercise, this person can help. Or if you are very low weight, you may need to stop exercising and, in consultation with your physician, decide when exercise can be started again. The goal is to give up compulsive and excessive exercise and learn how to develop a healthy lifestyle of activity.

A psychiatrist (M.D.)

If you, your physician or therapist decides medication may be helpful, a psychiatrist can prescribe what you need. The decision to use medication has to be carefully considered because of the complications of low weight and other factors. Sometimes tagalong conditions like depression and anxiety may bring up the question of medication use. Medications may be used to improve mood, control urges to binge and deal with excessive anxiety.

An individual therapist

It is helpful to find someone who has experience working with eating disorders. This person is usually a mental health practitioner—a psychologist, clinical social worker, marriage and family therapist, professional counselor or pastoral counselor. The therapist helps you deal with underlying emotional, spiritual and interpersonal issues that are playing out through preoccupation with food. The focus is usually self-examination and identification of thoughts and behaviors that need change. The goal is to help you develop better eating habits, understand the triggers for binges and food restriction and make changes where needed.

A *family therapist*

Family work is so important because families influence the development and maintenance of eating problems. It is especially needed with young girls and teens and highly recommended for all types of eating problems. You are responsible for your actions, but families play a role in maintaining symptoms. Family work can strengthen the marital couple's relationship, help parents know how to react to eating problems and know how to intervene, bring siblings together, help you develop a more independent self while still being part of your family and help you launch from the family system in a healthy way.

A group therapist

Some people are helped by attending a group that is supportive, provides information or is a safe place to practice new skills. If you join a group therapy, you can work on relationships with other people and share your struggles with those who have similar issues. Group members usually help you feel less isolated, less ashamed and more supported. Many groups provide good information along with support. Therapy groups can assist you in the practice of assertiveness, help you find your voice and identity and explore interpersonal issues. I recommend you find groups led by trained professionals and who will integrate your faith with treatment.

At this point, you may be thinking, *Wow! This sounds like involving a lot of people in my life and feels a little overwhelming.* It is a lot of people, but they all have roles to play in helping you get better. Remember these disorders do damage to the physical body; therefore, someone who is qualified to monitor your health needs to be involved. And you need to learn to eat properly and not use food as a numbing agent or escape from life's problems. If you don't want to stay sick, you have to find your true identity, face your growing independence and deal more effectively with relationships.

MEDICATION

Let's talk briefly about the use of medication. As I mentioned, medication is not a given. Many of my clients are helped without ever using medication. However, medication isn't wrong to use. Keep in mind that medication doesn't cure anything. It helps manage symptoms. Symptom management can be a short-term goal. The

God is our source of healing, but He allows us to use modern medicine in the process.

long-term goal is to be free of the disorder.

The use of medication is considered case by case and involves a number of factors, including the state of your health. If medication is recommended, discuss with the physician and therapist why you would use it, the potential side effects and how this fits into the long-term goal of freedom. Then pray about the decision. There is nothing sinful about taking medications, and doing so doesn't mean you lack faith. I say this because so many Christians feel condemned about taking medication when it comes to emotional problems. Yet, these agents often help a person think clearer and function better. God is our source of healing, but He allows us to use modern medicine in the process. Continue to trust Him for total healing.

Setting a Healthy Weight Goal

It is important to set two weight goals. The first weight goal is called an *ideal* weight. Determine your ideal weight by locating the numbers on the most recent health insurance charts that provide weight ranges according to your height and body frame size. This is a fast and easy way to know what is considered a healthy range in terms of weight. Long term, you want to stay within this healthy weight range.

The second weight goal is called a *target weight*. The target weight is considered the lowest possible medically safe weight. An easy way to figure this weight is to take 90 percent of the midpoint of the ideal body range. The physician and dietitian should have input regarding this number, but once it is set, it doesn't change. It is not a magic number, but does indicate a bottom-line weight to stay above. It is needed because of the physical damage that comes from too low a weight. Once the number is set, negotiations should cease. Why? Because when the eating disorder is active, women engage in power struggles over the number, constantly trying to renegotiate it, related to the need for control.

Once you know the ideal and target weights for your body type and height, you have concrete goals to guide you. They are meant to help you stay out of medical trouble and provide you with reasonable parameters. The sooner you stop fighting the numbers, the faster you will face the issues that underlie the weight struggle. That's where real freedom begins.

Overall, the road to freedom is usually a team effort (quarterbacked by God), using the resources of many fields. Remember, the earlier you intervene, the easier it is to make changes. And once you admit to the problem, commit to change and surrender your will to God's, there is hope.

BREAKING 🦅 F R E E
PRAYER FOR YOU

Lord, I've prided myself on self-sufficiency. I thought it was weak to need help with this problem. I realize I need other people to help me. Forgive my self-dependency. Lead me to the people who can help, and teach me Your ways in this entire process. Help me to give up trying to control everything.

CHAPTER 5

BREAK-FREE STRATEGIES

For many, negative thinking is a habit, which over time becomes an addiction. A lot of people suffer from this disease because negative thinking is addictive to each of the Big Three—the mind, the body and the emotions. If one doesn't get you, the others are waiting in the wings.

—PETER MCWILLIAMS

*I*t is possible to break free from an eating disorder. The first two steps of the process were discussed in previous chapters. They are:

- Admit you have a problem. This requires confronting the denial you have allowed to operate.

- Be willing to get help. Start the

process with a physical examination from your doctor.

If necessary, allow others to take part in
your healing and restoration. God wants
to heal all the parts of you, not just a few
symptoms. Be willing to do whatever it
takes.

SYMPTOM TRACKING

It's easy to think only about the eating
symptoms. After all, food obsession,
restriction, bingeing and purging occupy
most of your thoughts and time. But these
symptoms are not the primary problem.
They are representative of other underlying emotional and spiritual issues. So you
have to find ways to connect the eating
symptoms to these underlying issues.

One way to do this is to track what
occurs *before* and *after* a problematic eating behavior (such as bingeing, purging or
food restriction). Typically, there is a situation, event, emotion or thought that sets
off an eating episode. You will want to
identify these *cues* or *triggers*. Once you
do, you can anticipate them and substitute

a new way to respond.

Use this simple tracking form. Write down when you last binged, purged or restricted food under the column *Behavior*. Next, identify what was happening at the time or right before you engaged in the behavior. Write down a brief description of this under the column *Situation*. Then write down what you felt at the time under *Emotion*. Finally, what thought automatically came into your head? Don't edit the thought. Just write down what came to mind under *Thought*. Examples are provided with the chart.

As you write down specific events and situations, emotions and thoughts, you will begin to see the cues that set off your eating symptoms. Typically, a pattern emerges.

For example, Alice noticed that every time she had a meeting with her boss, she restricted food. Something about those meetings bothered her. Before she kept the tracking chart, she never noticed the connection: food restriction and meetings with her boss. The felt emotion was fear, and her automatic thought was, *He doesn't like me.*

Since Alice didn't want to change jobs, she decided to work on the fear and negative thought. Fear of man is not healthy. So Alice prayed for forgiveness. Only God is to be feared, and He is the source of her provision and supply, not her boss. She was competently doing her job, so her worry was unreasonable. She prayed to be released from the fear of this man who, incidentally, reminded her of her abusive father. She then worked on the real source of her fear—her relationship with her father.

Next, she examined her thought. Was *being liked* the goal of her employment? Yes, it's nice when the boss likes you, but she had done nothing to make him *not* like her. Her thought was irrational. But what if she was right, and he didn't like her? Since she had done nothing to bring on the dislike, she had no control over how he felt about her anyway. Food restricting solved nothing. It was a false sense of control and a response to her insecure feelings. In counseling, she worked on not giving others the power to define her. Again, she realized that her fear about being liked began when

Tracking My Food Triggers

Behavior	Situation	Emotion	Thought
Binged/purged	Break up with boyfriend	Hurt	I'll never be loved.
Food restricted	Friend made nasty comment	Angry	I can't compete with her.

her dad verbally and physically abused her. She was transferring that fear to other males in authority over her. If she wanted freedom, she would have to tackle the lies associated with her original wounding.

If you use this chart to track your symptoms for a few weeks, you'll begin to see the necessity for renewed thinking and new responses to emotional issues. You will identify lies you have believed. In addition, the underlying causes of your food problems will become more apparent. Then you can work on those issues and not focus so intently on the eating behavior. You won't be ignoring the eating problems because those bad habits must be changed, but you will begin to see that those habits represent other emotional, relational and spiritual issues.

FREE YOURSELF FROM CULTURAL PRESCRIPTIONS OF BEAUTY AND BODY IMAGE

Our preoccupation with looking beautiful prevents us from dealing with more difficult aspects of life. It's easier, for example, to redo a hairstyle five times than resolve conflict with a mother. You can spend time shopping for shoes but find it difficult to relax. The art of makeup can be mastered far before you master stress.

You only have one body to work with while on earth. You can hate it and make it your enemy, or you can take care of it and develop other parts of your character. Body obsession keeps you distracted. You can blame everything on your weight and not face your problems. Outer beauty can be a mask that hides a deeper insecurity. Instead of spending time painstakingly measuring food, use that time to become more intimate with God. He loves you unconditionally and doesn't care what you look like on the outside. He wants your time to be devoted to things that bring eternal significance. He doesn't want you to waste time hating a body that never measures up to some temporal, cultural standard.

Our cultural prescriptions of beauty aren't in line with what God says is important. God looks at the inner person. He sees our heart and wants our devotion to be to Him. The Bible has answers to what constitutes inner beauty. Work on your Christlike character.

Stop poring over fashion magazines and filling your eyes with unrealistic images. In addition, ask family members and friends to stop commenting on appearances. Kindly tell them you are trying to break free from body obsession. You prefer that their conversation center on other qualities of people—character, kindness, patience, good deeds and such things. This may require you to be assertive! (See page 72.)

Our cultural prescriptions of beauty aren't in line with what God says is important.

DEVELOP HEALTHY EATING HABITS

Food is not bad. It is a source of nourishment and enjoyment and needs to be restored to those ends. You've developed habits and thoughts that need changing when it comes to food choices, amounts and calories. Don't skip meals. Work with a dietitian who can help you gain weight slowly and safely and/or stop bingeing. And remember, the 24/7 food obsession is preventing you from dealing with the true source of your pain. The longer you hold on to unhealthy eating patterns, the longer you will stay in bondage to the disorder. Freedom requires an act of your will. Decide to eat differently. At first, it won't feel comfortable, but don't go by your feelings.

TAKE OFF THE MASK

You may be old enough to remember former lead singer of The Doors, Jim Morrison. Despite his musical genius, he was a tormented soul. He spoke to the difficulty of unmasking the true self.

> Most people love you for who you pretend to be…To keep their love, you keep pretending—performing. You get to love your pretense…It's true, we're locked in an image, an act. And the sad thing is, people get so used to their image—they grow attached to their masks. They love their chains. They forget all about who they really are. And, if you try to remind them, they hate you for it. They feel like you're trying to steal their most precious possession.[1]

It's easy to get locked into an image. People may see you as someone who has it all together and not know the internal pain you feel. You don't have to keep pretending. Take off the mask. You won't be hated for it. Jesus loves you no matter what is underneath. Don't be afraid. He already knows what's there! He sees your weaknesses and loves you anyway. Just be real with Him. Don't love the chains of this bondage. Christ wants to set you free.

DEVELOP REALISTIC EXPECTATIONS

Unrealistic expectations are a setup for failure. You can't do everything without exhausting yourself and losing balance in life. In the biblical story of Mary and Martha, Martha could not continue serving Jesus and listen at His feet. She had to stop one thing to do another. You are no different. Stop the constant performance, and learn to rest and have down time. This is probably one of the hardest directives for someone with an eating disorder because you feel driven. Practice relaxation. I recommend *Breaking Free From Stress* as a guide to help you slow down and learn to relax.[2] No one's body can handle a constant state of performance. Rest is needed.

Stop Trying to Be Perfect

There was only one perfect person. He was Jesus. You will not attain perfection on this earth no matter how hard you try. You are under construction, and the finished product won't be realized in this lifetime. So stop pushing yourself to a goal that is unrealistic. Perfection, even if it was possible, wouldn't win you love or acceptance.

We are all flawed and in need of the redemption of Jesus Christ. In our weakness He becomes strong. If you believe perfection is needed to win approval or affection, this is a lie. Renounce this belief. You already have both in Christ. Nothing you did won that affection. Ask God to reveal this truth to you.

Find Your Voice

The hard but necessary work is to find your own voice. It has been lost in the sea of other people's thoughts and opinions.

Stop trying to be what you think others want you to be, and start defining who you are. What do you think, feel and believe? Your identity development was arrested when the eating disorder began. Instead of testing out your own voice, you did what you thought pleased others. Now you have to learn who you are in Christ and move confidently in that identity.

Examine your motives, true feelings and thoughts. This self-definition is a necessary step in maturation. If you don't like what you see, that's OK, because God will help change you. The Holy Spirit will empower you to be more like Christ. Imitate Him as you allow the Holy Spirit to renew your mind and guard your heart.

PRACTICE ASSERTIVENESS SKILLS

Once you find your voice, practice using it. This often requires asserting your opinion or belief. In my experience, those who struggle with anorexia tend to be too passive. Those with bulimia tend to be too aggressive. Often, assertiveness training is needed.

People cannot read your mind even

though you wish they could. So it is up to you to learn to be more assertive in order to meet your needs, set limits and take charge of your life where and when you can. If you've never learned this skill and are unsure how to be assertive, here is a step-by-step description.

MENTAL HEALTH FACT

Develop Assertiveness Skills

- *Evaluate the situation.* Do you really want to do what is being asked? Do you like the way things are going? Do you need to speak up because you are bothered? If you don't act, will you feel resentful, upset, anxious or down? Decide if this is a time to speak up.

- *Timing is important.* Decide *when* you need to address an issue. Should you speak up immediately, or do you need time to think about how you feel and the consequences of addressing the situation now?

Perhaps you want to organize your thoughts, decide if you are reacting to the right issue or need to build courage.

Knowing *when* to confront is important. For example, asserting yourself when you are really angry is not a good idea. It would be better to take a time-out, identify what you are reacting to and practice a calm way to address the issue rather than impulsively lash out and say things you may later regret (an emotional binge).

- *Identify the problem.* Be specific. Don't expect others to read your mind or magically to guess your distress. Say exactly what the problem is and how it is affecting you.

- *Say how you feel.* No one *causes* you to feel things. You allow yourself to feel things. So don't blame others. For example, instead of saying, "You make me so mad when you don't answer my question," say "I get upset when my question isn't answered. I feel ignored." The purpose is to communicate the feeling (from your point of view) associated with the behavior.

- *Say what you want to have happen.* This is the tough, but important part. You need to know what you want and what would help the situation. For example, "I worry when you don't come home from work on time. I start thinking all kinds of crazy things. So I would like you to call me if you are going to be late. That way I'll know nothing bad happened." It is important to communicate a solution or desire so that the other person has an idea how to remedy the problem. This doesn't guarantee that person will do what you request, but at least you've communicated what would help and can negotiate from there.

~~~~~~~~~~~~~~~~~~

Assertiveness requires practice. It gets easier the more you do it. The end result will be a more confident you.

One of the reasons we don't practice being assertive is because we don't know what we want. We are wishy-washy, unsure and undefined. We allow others to manipulate us into doing things and then feel resentful because we have too much to do. Or we feel guilty and don't believe we have the right to speak up. We ask, "Who am I to say no?" Speak up and let your voice be heard. When you address problems as they occur, you won't build up anger and hold on to things that can grow into resentment. Often times, this is a root of depression, anxiety and eating disorders.

Your mind is vulnerable if you don't renew it with the Word of God.

DAILY RENEW YOUR MIND

I can't say enough about the importance of this step. The enemy keeps you in bondage by deceiving you. He latches on to your weaknesses and attacks your thoughts. Your mind is vulnerable if you don't renew it with the Word of God. Daily put on your spiritual armor and fight negative thoughts. Because of the Holy Spirit in you, you have the power to overcome the attacks of the enemy. Take your position of victory and hold on to it every day.

Learn to take your thoughts captive. When a negative thought enters your mind, stop it and think about something else. Distract yourself by focusing on something positive or on a biblical truth. For example, if the thought *I need to be thinner* keeps entering your mind, stop and think, *This is not true. It is a lie implanted by the one who wants me destroyed. I won't listen to it. I know that God accepts me the way I am. Others who love me tell me that I don't need to lose any more weight. This thought must leave me now. God, thanks for loving me as I am.*

IDENTIFY AND EXPRESS FEELINGS

For some of you, knowing what you feel at any given time is a mystery. When asked how you feel about something, you go blank. You have not learned to identify your feelings, perhaps because you've turned them off and covered them up by focusing on food and weight.

The goal is to learn to identify feelings—happy ones and sad ones. When feelings are painful or negative, the tendency is to push them away or bury them deep inside. Instead, do the uncomfortable and express those feelings directly.

CONFRONT NEGATIVE FEELINGS

When you begin to identify feelings, many of them will be negative. The temptation is to swallow negative feelings or to pretend they don't exist. I often tell my anorexic clients they have pushed so many negative feelings inside there is no room for food. Negative feelings must be confronted and resolved. Conflict resolution is a learned and practiced skill.

BREAKING FREE
MENTAL HEALTH FACT

Learn to Problem Solve

Problem solving can also be taught. Here is the basic process:

- *Define the problem.* Get a clear definition as to what the actual difficulty may be. For example, when mealtime becomes tense, the problem isn't that your mother nags you. The problem is that you refuse to eat properly. Your behavior brings on the tension. So be specific and focus on the behavior. Then clearly define the behavior so you aren't working with some nebulous thing. If you specifically define the problem, you'll know what needs to change. In the example, eating a meal will get rid of the tension. Your mother won't have to nag because you have assumed responsibility.

- *How often or how long is the problem happening?* Measure the number of times the problem occurs or the length of time it goes on. This way you will have an accurate count or duration of the problem. This is important because you need to measure change. Too often we don't recognize small changes made in the right direction. If it feels like you are doing something *all the time*, measure it to see if this is true. It probably isn't.

- *Do something.* Time to intervene. Instead of acting the way you always do or in a way that doesn't promote change, try a new strategy. For example, instead of arguing with your mother over a meal portion, take the initiative to accurately learn about food portions with the dietitian. She can teach portion sizes using food models. Once you have an accurate understanding about portion sizes, your mother won't have to be the food police. In other words, stop doing the thing that doesn't work (arguing) and try a new tactic (taking responsibility). You can experiment until you find something that works.

- *Evaluate how well things are going.* If you have a clear definition of the problem, measure how much of a problem it is and then do something, you can see if the behavior gets better or worse or happens less or more.

Using the above example, if you choose your food portions wisely for two out of three meals, you've made progress. Change is usually a step-by-step process that requires patience.

- *If what you are doing doesn't work, try another tactic.* The secret is not to panic or give up when something you try doesn't work. Try something else. Talk to other people—family members or a counselor—and get input if you need it. Just because you don't see a solution doesn't mean there isn't one. There is always a way. Remember that this is also a promise from God. He makes a way where there is no way. So don't panic or give up.

Confronting negative feelings is particularly important when dealing with family members and friends. If you allow negativity to simmer inside, it will lead to more eating symptoms.

WORK ON ALL
YOUR RELATIONSHIPS

Relationship issues are key to breaking free from eating disorders. Usually there are so many fears about relationships, some born out of experience and others out of perceptions. One common fear is that you must give up your identity to be in relationship with someone else. This is so untrue. Relationships are best when each person knows who they are and can move confidently in their identity. Problems arise when you don't have any sense of this, or when you comply passively to what others want, not thinking for yourself.

In family relationships, the goal is to grow as your own separate person while staying in relationship with others. This means you work on developing a separate sense of who you are in the context of your family relationships. Finding your voice and becoming a separate individual doesn't

Relationships are best when each person knows who they are and can move confidently in their identity.

happen by cutting off family relationships. Nor is it a good idea to become overly dependent on family members for your emotional needs. A balance of separation and attachment is needed. For women with eating disorders, this process of growing up and becoming more independent is frightening. Sometimes there is a secret wish to stay childlike because maturation and budding sexuality can feel scary.

Growing up is not as frightening as it seems when guided by love. Your family may have to work together to learn how to set appropriate boundaries, be interdependent, deal with conflict, nurture each other in healthy ways and identify and express feelings.

In some families, relationships are so chaotic and unpredictable that they feel out of control. This is often the case in families with abuse, alcoholism or mental illness. In those cases, family work centers on stopping the dysfunction, setting appropriate boundaries and regulating feelings.

LOSE THE ALL-OR-NOTHING THINKING

A hallmark of an eating disorder is *all-or-nothing* thinking. Things are either all bad or all good. There is no middle ground or balance in thinking or behavior. Eating symptoms reflect this dichotomy—food restrict, binge-purge—there is no moderate eating, just the extremes.

Challenge your thinking. For example, when you make a mistake, don't think, I'*m a failure*. Instead think, *I messed up. OK, I'll try again*. Avoid words like *always, never, no one, everybody*—these are easy traps to make you feel discouraged and defeated.

STOP LIVING IN FEAR

Fear is not from God. It stops you from inheriting God's promises. Someone with an eating disorder fears getting fat and losing control. Second Timothy 1:7 reminds us, "For God hath not given us the spirit of fear; but of power, and of love, and of a sound mind" (KJV). Since fear is from the enemy, we need to "cast off the works of darkness, and let us put on the armour of light" (Rom.

13:12, KJV). Live in the truth of God's Word.

FACE YOUR EMERGING SEXUALITY

Your body and sexuality were created by God. But as we learned in previous chapters, our bodies are living sacrifices to God. "Therefore, I urge you, brothers, in view of God's mercy, to offer your bodies as living sacrifices, holy and pleasing to God—this is your spiritual act of worship" (Rom. 12:1). For the anorexic, the developing body is frightening. Sexuality represents out-of-control sensations and attention from the opposite sex. Instead of learning how to manage these impulses and attention, sexuality is denied through starvation. The body returns to childlike form. This reaction is based in fear and avoidance and is not healthy.

Bulimics tend to have trouble managing sexual impulses. Sexuality is not denied, but is often used to gain acceptance and approval. Impulses feel out of control and need to be contained. Be accountable to God for your sexual behavior. Once you are purchased by God, your body is no longer your own. Daily present your body as a living sacrifice. Live holy, and do not exploit the beautiful creation that you are.

Work Through Any Experience of Trauma or Loss

So often the roots of an eating disorder can be traced back to a trauma such as sexual abuse, rape, rejection or loss. You must grieve those experiences and believe God can redeem and restore what was stolen from you. Work through the emotions, feel them deeply and ask God to speak His truth into any lies that were implanted at the time of wounding or hurt. Don't be afraid to go to counseling to work on trauma and loss.

Regulate Your Emotions

Emotions come and go. Sometimes we feel them intensely. At other times we try to deny them because of the pain involved. If you suffer with an eating disorder, chances are you have difficulty regulating the emotions you feel. Like the all-or-nothing thinking, emotions tend to follow a similar pattern—intensely upset or numb. In order to break free, you must learn to control and contain your emotional states. If you are anorexic, you over control your emotions and restrict their expression (just like restricting food). If you are bulimic, you are impulsive and react intensely. You need to slow down and think before you respond.

IDENTIFY THE LIES YOU BELIEVE THAT KEEP YOU TRAPPED

Whenever we experience emotional pain, the enemy has an opportunity to lie to us. If he is successful at getting us to believe his falsehoods, he can keep us in distress. Once saved, we are the righteousness of Christ. The Bible doesn't say we *become* the righteousness of God. It says we *are*. Your spirit was made new at salvation, but your mind still needs renewing.

Have you listened to the enemy's voice telling you that you are worthless, hopeless, unlovable, rejected or not good enough? These are lies. Find the lie that keeps you symptomatic, and ask God to speak His truth to you concerning that lie. For example, if you have regular thoughts of being worthless, try to think back to when you first began to feel this way. Can you identify an experience, event or a time when you felt this feeling intensely? Allow yourself to feel that sense of worthlessness, and ask Jesus to speak truth into the situation. His truth can set you free of this lie.

Go to Him in prayer, and ask for His truth to be revealed in the dark places of your heart. Once you experience Him, you will be healed.

BREAKING FREE
PRAYER FOR YOU

I believe the truth can set me free. I want to be completely free from this bondage. Lord, You can do this in me. I will renew my mind daily, give my body as a living sacrifice, surrender to Your love and do my part in throwing off these chains of bondage. If I need to be more assertive, find my voice, practice relaxing or whatever it takes, I'm willing to do it. Empower me to make changes.

CHAPTER 6

BREAKING FREE SUMMARY

It's not that some people have willpower and some don't. It's that some people are ready to change and others are not.

—JAMES GORDON, M.D.

I like the above quote because it speaks to our willingness to change. This is so necessary in breaking free from an eating disorder. Engaging in eating symptoms may be tiring and destructive, but they are like an old friend, familiar!

God is your healer, but you have to cooperate with the healing process. He wants to do a deep work in you. Let Him.

Here is a brief review of the break-free steps:

1. Admit you have a problem. Confront your denial.

2. Ask for help. By faith, believe that you can be healed and your life different.

3. If necessary, be willing to work with a team of people who will address all aspects of the eating disorder.

4. Get a complete physical examination by a physician.

5. Track your symptoms in order to identify triggers and work on thoughts and emotional responses.

6. Be willing to look below the surface of eating problems for root causes.

7. Base your image and esteem in Christ.

8. Practice healthy eating patterns.

9. Set realistic goals and expectations.

10. Stop trying to be perfect.

11. Daily renew your mind.

12. Find your voice.

13. Directly express and confront negative feelings.

14. Practice assertiveness and problem solving.

15. Lose your "all-or-nothing" thinking.

16. Learn to regulate your emotions.

17. Stop living in fear.

18. Identify the lies that keep you trapped.

19. Face the normal developmental tasks of growing up—independence, budding sexuality, forming an identity and leaving home.

20. Resolve relationship issues. Begin with your family.

21. Work through trauma and loss and any other "tagalong" conditions.

THE HOPE

In [this] freedom Christ has made us free [and completely liberated us]; stand fast then, and do not be hampered and held ensnared and submit again to a yoke of slavery [which you have once put off].

—GALATIANS 5:1, AMP

Over the past fifteen years I've worked for a number of programs that treat eating disorders. The goal in most of these programs is recovery from the eating disorder. Recovery usually includes a return to healthy eating and an absence of symptoms. After treatment, many report a lapse or feel that food struggles will always be with them to some degree. While recovery is a good goal, there is something much better. It's called *complete freedom*.

Is it realistic to expect that complete freedom is possible? Yes, because of Christ and the Holy Spirit working within us, freedom from all aspects of these disorders is possible. You don't have to live the rest of your life wondering if and when the eating symptoms may recur, or if the distorted body image will ever go away, or if you'll ever eat "normally" again. Don't settle for recovery or improvement. Ask God to set you free, and allow the Holy Spirit to work in you.

When you struggle with this thing that seems more powerful than you, remember that the cross defeated it. In Galatians 5:17, Paul reminds us that our flesh and spirit are in constant conflict. The two war against each other.

If you still feel hopeless, remember that God promised you a way out.

Our spirit is made new at salvation, but our mind needs constant renewal and our flesh must be crucified in obedience to God's plan. If we submit to the Holy Spirit's control and die to flesh, the eating disorder can be broken. The vigilance once directed toward food control can be redirected to putting on the armor of God.

The temptation is to trust your own strength or abilities even though you've proven over and over that this doesn't work. It's hard to give up what is familiar and to move into the unknown. But the new journey will prove fruitful.

So, if you feel defeated or as though you can't overcome this all-consuming force in your life, let 1 Corinthians 10:13 encourage you. I like to read it in the Amplified Bible.

> For no temptation (no trial regarded as enticing to sin, no matter how it comes or where it leads) has overtaken you and laid hold on you that is not common to man [that is, no temptation or trial has come to you that is beyond human resistance and that is not adjusted and adapted and belonging to human experience, and such as man can bear]. But God is faithful [to His Word and to His compassionate nature], and He [can be trusted] not to let you be tempted and tried and assayed beyond your ability and strength of resistance and power to endure, but with the temptation He will [always] also pro-

vide the way out (the means of escape to a landing place), that you may be capable and strong and powerful to bear up under it patiently.

Paul's word to us is that God is faithful and can be trusted. What good news! And He ALWAYS provides a way out. If you still feel hopeless, remember that God promised you a way out.

It's time to arm yourself for the battle. You will be victorious, but you must prepare by putting on the full armor of God.

Finally, be strong in the Lord and in his mighty power. Put on the full armor of God so that you can take your stand against the devil's schemes. For our struggle is not against flesh and blood, but against the rulers, against the authorities, against the powers of this dark world and against the spiritual forces of evil in the heavenly realms. Therefore put on the full armor of God, so that when the day of evil comes, you may be able to stand your ground, and after you have done everything, to stand.

—EPHESIANS 6:10–13

Prepare yourself. Trust Him. Put on the mind of Christ. You have nothing to lose. Be strong and be patient. You will break free!

BREAKING FREE
PRAYER FOR YOU

Lord, thank You for providing a way out of this struggle. I do trust You to heal me completely. I don't want to deal with this for the rest of my life. I want freedom today. You alone are my strength and shield, a present help in my time of trouble. I will put on the mind of Christ, arm myself for battle and go forward in victory!

NOTES

CHAPTER 1

1. Mary Kay Blakely, *American Mom: Motherhood, Politics, and Humble Pie* (Chapel Hill, NC: Algonquin Books, 1994), prologue.
2. W. S. Agras, "The eating disorders," *Scientific American Medicine*, vol. 3, D. C. Dale and D. D. Federman, eds. (New York: Scientific American, 2001), 1–7. "Eating Disorders," *Diagnostic and Statistical Manual of Mental Disorders*, 4th ed. (Washington, DC: American Psychiatric Association, 2000).
3. "Eating Disorders," *Diagnostic and Statistical Manual of Mental Disorders*.
4. Ibid. See also WebMD Health Online. Anorexia: Other physical symptoms of Anorexia Nervosa associated with starvation. Retrieved online July 13, 02 from http://my.webmd.com/encyclopedia/article/4115.15255#hw44987.
5. "Eating Disorders," *Diagnostic and Statistical Manual of Mental Disorders*.
6. "Eating disorders," pamphlet produced by the APA Joint Commission on Public Affairs and the Division of Public Affairs, 1996.
7. Something Fishy Website on Eating

Disorders. *Issues for men with eating disorders*. Retrieved online July 14, 02 from www.somethingfishy.org/cultural/issues-formen.php.

8. Arnold Andersen, "Eating disorders in males," in *Eating Disorders and Obesity*, Kelly Brownell and Christopher Fairburn, eds. (New York: The Guilford Press, 1995).

9. Margo Maine, Ph.D., "Clinical Update: Eating Disorders," a supplement to the *Family Therapy News*, vol. 1, Issue 6 (November 1999): AAMFT.

10. Ibid.

CHAPTER 2

1. Maine, "Clinical Update: Eating Disorders," *Family Therapy News*.

CHAPTER 3

1. Linda S. Mintle, Ph.D., *Breaking Free From a Negative Self-Image* (Lake Mary, FL: Charisma House, 2002).

CHAPTER 5

1. Online dictionary of quotations. Retrieved July 11, 2002 from www.quotationreference.com.

2. Linda S. Mintle, Ph.D., *Breaking Free From Stress* (Lake Mary, FL: Charisma House, 2002).

Your Walk With God Can Be Even Deeper...

With *Charisma* magazine, you'll be informed and inspired by the features and stories about what the Holy Spirit is doing in the lives of believers today.

Each issue:

- Brings you exclusive world-wide reports to rejoice over.
- Keeps you informed on the latest news from a Christian perspective.
- Includes miracle-filled testimonies to build your faith.
- Gives you access to relevant teaching and exhortation from the most respected Christian leaders of our day.

Call 1-800-829-3346 for 3 FREE trial issues
Offer #A2CCHB

If you like what you see, then pay the invoice of $22.97 (**saving over 51% off the cover price**) and receive 9 more issues (12 in all). Otherwise, write "cancel" on the invoice, return it, and owe nothing.

Experience the Power of Spirit-Led Living

Charisma Offer #A2CCHB
P.O. Box 420234
Palm Coast, Florida 32142-0234
www.charismamag.com

2577